Ten Waltzes

by Johann Strauss, Jr. for Solo Piano

By Gail Smith

A recording of the music in this book is now available. The publisher strongly recommends the use of this recording along with the text to insure accuracy of interpretation and ease in learning.

CONTENTS

'A Sketch at a Ball'
From 'Mr. Chumley's Holidays' by Randolph Caldecott
Coloured lithograph, 1883

FOREWORD

Around the mid-18th Century the stage was set for the waltz to take over the role of the minuet and become the foremost dance of a whole age. The Viennese waltz in its classic form was known as a whirling or revolving dance with the characteristic feature being a swift tempo.

At that time it was fashionable to be a virtuoso dancer, to waltz with one's partner from one corner of the hall to the opposite corner in the most rapid tempo. In Vienna there were dancing palaces which were magnificent and enormous in size, having no equal in all of Europe. The Apollo Palace was such a place. It contained 5 large and 31 smaller dancing rooms in which balls for 6,000 persons at a time could be given.

The waltz was danced with a passion that had never been seen before in a dance. People found it irresistible. The dance craze of Vienna was contagious. In 1832 no less than 772 balls were given, attended by 200,000 guests, nearly half the total population of Vienna!

Among the composers of waltzes were Schubert, Chopin, Beethoven, and Mozart, but Haydn composed the very first one for piano. Musically speaking, the waltz owes its development to Weber, who adopted the waltz form and prepared the way for the stream of waltzes in the 19th Century. Johann Strauss the elder introduced the habit of giving names to waltzes. It was at Vienna, under the Strauss family, Lanner, Labitzky and Gung'l, that the waltz became fixed in the form in which we know it now, with an introduction generally in a slow tempo (which was composed to give the dancers time to arrange themselves in couples), followed by five or six waltzes ending with a coda recapitulating the best waltzes.

The undisputed "Waltz King" was Johann Strauss, Jr., who was born in Vienna on October 25, 1825, and died there on June 3, 1899. He composed nearly 400 waltzes. His father had composed 152 waltzes.

The waltz affects listeners of every generation, and one writer put it this way: "those irresistible waltzes that first catch the ear, and then curl round the heart, till on a sudden they invade and will have the legs."

Studies have shown that listening to waltz music produces a feeling of well-being. The selections in this book have been chosen from the hundreds of waltzes that Johann Strauss composed. These are the ten most beautiful, charming, lovely waltzes in all the world. Enjoy!

Gail Smith

VOICES OF SPRING

Frühlingsstimmen

Johann Strauss, Op. 410

p
f
mf
f
tr
f
mf

f
f
tr
f
mf
mf

dolce
f
p
mf
dolce
f
p
mf
f
p
f

f
p dolce
f
f
tr
f
tr
p dolce

f
poco ritard.
p
f
a tempo
f
p
f
sf
f

p
f
sf
f
p dolce
poco ritard.
a tempo
mf
tr
tr
tr
p

poco meno
tr
mf
p
pp
p dolce
pp
1.
2.
p dolce
poco rit.
fz
poco rit.

a tempo
fz poco rit.
a tempo
1.
2.
fz poco rit.
Coda
f

tr
tr
tr
tr
p
f
mf
mf
dolce
f
p
mf
dolce
f
p
mf

f
p
f
p
p
p dolce
tr

tr
p dolce
Cadenza ad lib.
1
pp
f
ff
fz

VIENNA LIFE

Wiener Blut
Walzer

Johann Strauss, Op. 354

Ped.
* Ped.
* Ped.
* Ped.
* Ped.
*
pp
f rit.
p
Tempo di Valse
fz
fz
fz
fz
p
pp

Walzer
1
p
p
sempre cresc.
f

1.
Fine
f
p
f
p
f
D.S.𝄋 al Fine
f
p
2
f
p

1.
2.
f
p
p
cresc.
f
1.
2.
Fine
p
p
D.S.

3.
f
p
p
cresc.
f
1.
2.
p
f
f
ff
rit. pp

a tempo
cresc.
f
f
fz
1.
2.
Fine
f
p
D.S.
4
f
p
p
f
1.
p

2.
f
ff
1.
2.
f
Coda
p
cresc.
più cresc.
f

p
p
pp
cresc.
Ped.
* Ped.
* Ped.

Ped.
*
*
p
mf
sempre cresc.
f
p

fz
Ped.
*
fz
Ped.
*
Ped.
ff
8va
fz
Ped.
*
(8va)
ff
fz

JOHANN STRAUSS THE YOUNGER
Painting by Franz von Lenbach, 1895

ARTISTS' LIFE

Künstlerleben
Walzer

Johann Strauss, Op. 316

Tempo di valse
pp
pp
pp
f
f
f
Walzer
1
p
p
p

pp
f
p
pp
pp
fz
mf

mf
f
1.
2.
Fine
mf
p
D.S.
2
p
p
cresc.
f
pp

p
cresc.
f
pp
f
p
p
pp

1.
2.
Fine
D.S.
3

tr
1.
2.
f
p
4

p
f
p
f
1.
2.
5
f
p ritard. a tempo
p
f

D.S. al Fine
1.
2.
Coda

pp
p
pp
p
f

f
p
pp
f
fz
tr
f

tr
f
p
f
p
tr

tr
tr
p
pp
f
p
pp
pp

f
p
p
(p)
f
sf
f
ff
Ped.
*

EMPEROR WALTZ

Kaiser-Waltz

Introduction

Johann Strauss, Op. 437

tr
tr
p legato
pp
cresc.
f
tr
p
tr

dim.
p
p
dim.
pp
cresc.
f
ff
sf
p espress.
Tempo di valse (𝅗𝅥. = 𝅝)
ritard.

1

fz
dim.
pp sempre legato
mf
p
pp
ff

2
p
f
mf
p
pp

f
fz
p legg.
f
fz
p
f
tr
3
f
p
mf

sempre ben marcato
ff
marc. molto
fz
fz

4
f
m.s.
f
m.s.
m.s.
1.
2.
fz
mf

ff
f
D.S.𝄋 al Coda ⊕
tr

Coda
p
cresc.
cresc. sempre
f
p
pp
mf legato espr.

mfz
p
f
fz
p

p
f
5
p
fz
f

ff
sempre ben marcato
f
ff molto marc.

fz
fz
p
molto ritenuto
p
a tempo
pp trem.
mp espress.

mf ritard.
p
molto rit.
tr
a tempo f
cresc.
ff
5
3
2
trem.

WINE, WOMEN AND SONG

Wein, Weib und Gesang

Walzer

Introduction

Johann Strauss, Op. 333

pp
p
f
Ped.
pp
fz
Ped.
*
Ped.
*
Ped.

f
*
p
rit.
Allegro moderato
p

f
f
f
cresc.
f
ff
p

tr
tr
f
ff
Maestoso
ff
Ped.

Tempo di valse
p
p
f
mf
Walzer
mf
14

ff
fz
fz
f
ff
p
1.
2.
Fine
f
mf
D.S.

2
f
pp
pp
ff
pp
pp
1.
2.
Fine
f
dolce
p

1.
2.
D.S.𝄋 al Fine
3
f
pp
p

f
fz
1.
2.
p
f
p
f
f
f

1.
2.
Fine
f
p
D.S.
4

1.
2.
D.S.𝄋 al Coda
To Coda
1.
2.
Coda
Ped.

THE KISS WALTZ

Kuß - Walzer

Lustige Kriteg

Introduction

Johann Strauss, Op. 400

1881

tr
Andantino
p
p
rit.
Walzer
(Nur für Natur)
p
dim.
p
p
p

(Ihr Cousin)
dim.
p

p
p
p
rit.
p a tempo
dim.
p

(Piff, paff, puff)
poco rit.
a tempo

rit.
f
fz
fz
p
p
p
dim.
p

p
dim.
p
(Herr Herzog)
f
p poco rit.
f
fz
1.
p poco rit.
2.
mf

p
mf
1.
2.
fz
p
f
p poco rit.
a tempo
p

f
f
fz
fz
p
dim.
p
p

dim.
p
p
p
p
p
p
p
p
p
p
p

rit.
mf a tempo
dim.
p
ff

8va
ff
8va
sf
fz
fz
Ped.
*

A GROUP OF WALTZERS
Coloured lithograph by J. H. A. Randal, 1817

TALES FROM THE VIENNA WOODS

Geschichten aus dem Wienerwald

Walzer

In this beautiful waltz, "Tales from the Vienna Woods", Johann Strauss paints a musical picture of the lovely wooded hills, the trees, the brooks, the flowers and the meadows that were near Vienna.

Johann Strauss, Op. 325

Introduction

Tempo di valse

p *f*

p

f

p *f*

p

p
f
f
lunga

Più lento
p
fp
fp
pp
Ped.
*
Fermate
tr
Moderato langsam (Ländlertempo)
p
pp

ppp
Bewegter
p
rit.
p
Vivace
Tempo di Valse
f
tr
fz
Tempo di Valse
p
Ped.

Walzer
1
poco rit.
f
pp

a tempo
cresc.
f
fz
1.
Fine
p
D.S.
2
p
p
p
mf

p
f
pp
1.
2.
p
cresc.
mf
f
1.
2.
Fine
D.S.

3
p
p
f
pp
1.
2.
Fine
p
mf
mf
1.
mf

2.
D.S.𝄋 al Fine
f
f
p
4
p
p
1.
2.
p
f
mf

f
p dolce
cresc.
tr
f
1.
Fine
p
D.S.

5
mf
f
pp
f
1.
2.
mf
mf
Fine
mf

fz
1.
2.
D.S.𝄋 al Fine
f
mf
𝄌 Coda
p
cresc.

f
ff
tr
p
p
p
Ped.
*
p

f
pp poco rit.

a tempo
cresc.
f
fz
p
p
Ped.
*
Ped.
*
Ped.
*

p
p
mf
f
p
f
f
f
f
ff

NB. Beim Tanz bleiben die Takte von
A bis B weg
A
fz
fz
fz
p
pp rit.
pp molto rit.
una corda
pp
pp
rit.
B (Walzer)
p a tempo
f tremolo

YOU AND YOU

Du und Du

Walzer nach Motiven der Operette: "Die Fledermaus!"

Poco animato
fz
fz
tr
tr
ff
f
p

Walzer
1
fz
mf
fz
ff
Fine
f

f
D.S. 𝄋 al Fine
Ped.
*
2
f
p
p

1.
2.
Fine
p
mf
fz
f

fz
p
D.S. 𝄋 al Fine
p
3
f
p
f

tr
mf
fz
f
p
mf
p
mf
f
Ped.
*
Ped.
*

p
pp
ppp
pp
mf
p
mf
p
mf
f
p
Ped.
*
Ped.
*
pp
mf
f
Ped.
*
1.
2.
ff
p
D.S.
Ped.
*

Coda
p
fz
p
f
fz
Ped.

fz
fz
p
*
cresc.
p
mf
f

f
f
Ped.
*
f

fz
p
fz
mf
fz
ff
ff
Ped.
*
Ped.
*
Ped.
*
Ped.
*
Ped.

Ped.
Ped.
f
ff
Ped.

An der schönen blauen Donau
Johann Strauss

THE BEAUTIFUL BLUE DANUBE

An der schönen blauen Donau

Walzer

When Franz Lizst was playing in the Vatican for the Pope, we are told he started out with a Bach fugue, then some variations, then Lizst played "The Blue Danube Waltz".

Introduction

Johann Strauss, Op. 314

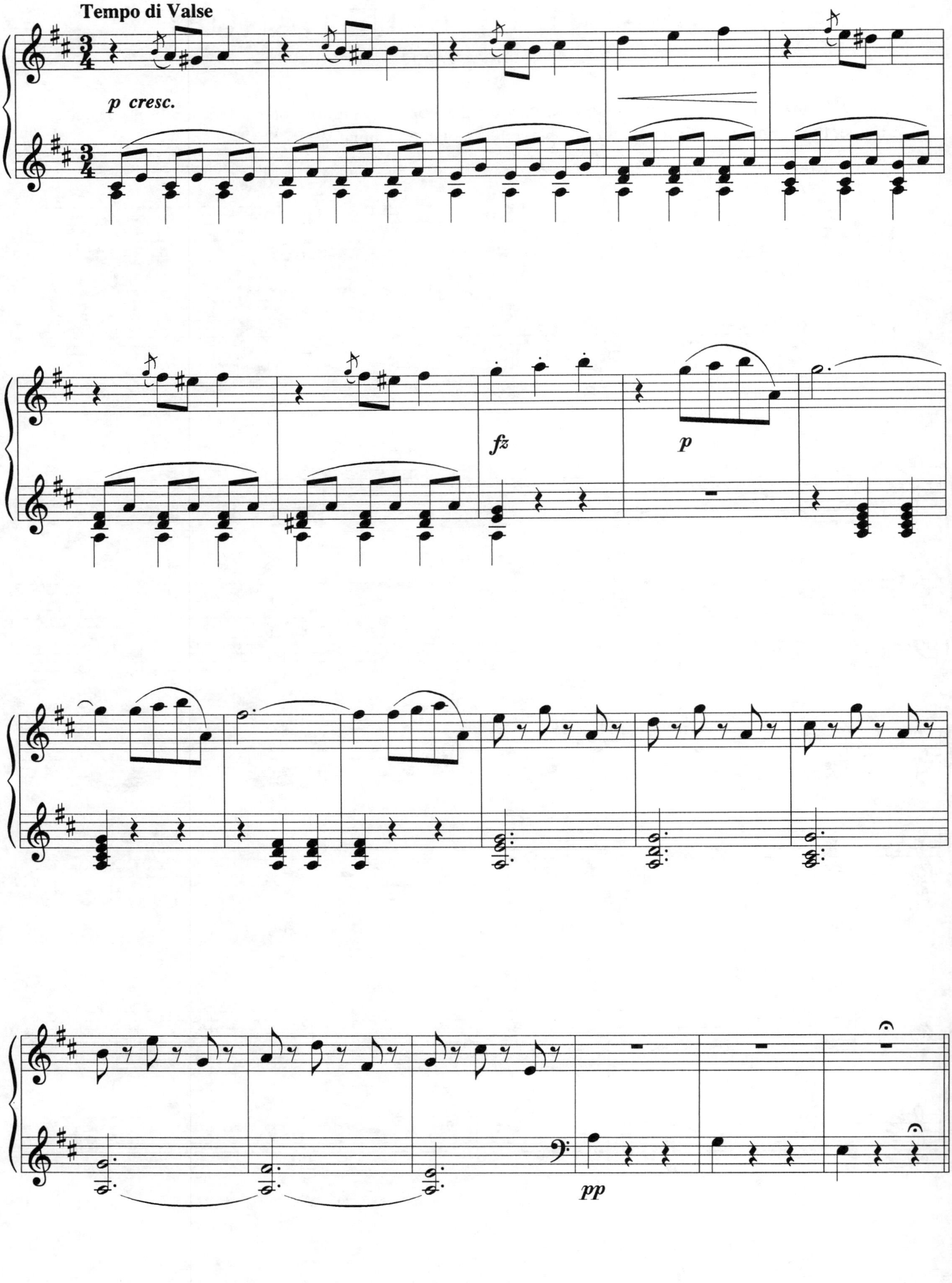

Tempo di Valse

p cresc.

fz

p

Walzer
1
p
f
ff

fz
fz
p
p
f
p
f
f
1.
2.
tr
Fine
p
D.S.
2
mf

1.
mf
2.
Fine
p
dolce
f
D.S.𝄋 senza repetizione
pp
mf
p

3
p
p
p cresc.
f
1.
2.
p
Lebhaft
p
fz
1.
2.
Fine
p
p
D.S.

4
1.
2.
tr

f
1.
2.
Fine
f
p
D.S.
5
f
p
p
f
p

p
1.
2.
f
pp

f
ff
To Coda
1.
Fine
p
D.S.
1. Coda Schluß bei Aufführung der Walzer mit Chor

2. Coda

p
f
f
tr
pp
p

tr
cresc.
f
pp
Ped.
*
Ped.
*
Ped.
*

cresc.
Ped.
*
f
Ped.
*
Ped.
*
ff
fz
fz
p
p

tr
pp
dimin.
tr
cresc.
f

'MORNING PAPERS'

Title-page of the waltz by Johann Strauss jun.

MORNING LEAVES

Morgenblätter
Walzer

The title is a pun on the German *Blatter,* meaning both "leaves" and "newspapers". Johann Strauss wrote this waltz for Vienna's journalists' association, Concordia.

Tempo di Valse
f
p
Walzer
1
p
p
tr
sfz

p
cresc.
f
Fine
p

1.
p
2.
p
p
D.C. al Fine
2
p

sfz
Fine
p
p
f
1.
2.
D.S.𝄋 al Fine
p
p

3
p
Fine
f

1.
2.
D.S.𝄋 al Fine
4
p
p
1.
Fine
2.
f
f

1.
2.
D.C. al Fine
f
5
f

1.
Fine
2.
f
p
p
f
pp
pp
1.
2.
D.S.𝄋 al Fine
p
f
Coda
p
p

f
f
p
p

sfz
p

pp
f
pp
p
tr
p

f
p
cresc.
f

ff
tr
tr